La Interseccion

poems by

Jennifer Mariela Rivera

Finishing Line Press
Georgetown, Kentucky

La Interseccion

A collection of poems that intersect the process of identification. Diving into the different fragments of a person's self-conscious while constructing the boundaries that society imposes on the individual.

Copyright © 2021 by Jennifer Mariela Rivera
ISBN 978-1-64662-647-2 First Edition
All rights reserved under International and Pan-American Copyright Conventions. No part of this book may be reproduced in any manner whatsoever without written permission from the publisher, except in the case of brief quotations embodied in critical articles and reviews.

ACKNOWLEDGMENTS

I could not have accomplished this without the professors that introduced me to various forms of poetry and literature. The English departments at Miami-Dade College and Florida International University are both full of professors that genuinely care about the students and actually take the time to teach their vocation.

I especially want to thank my partner, Carlos Arrocha, for continuously pushing me to follow my passion. Even though I am always terribly shy when it comes to sharing my writing with you.

I also want to thank my younger brother Ruben, for being the most loving and adoring younger sibling I could ask for and for helping me become the woman I am today. The bond that we forged based on acceptance and love allowed me to indulge and create something I truly I am proud of.

Publisher: Leah Huete de Maines
Editor: Christen Kincaid
Cover Art: Carlos Arrocha/Photographer
Author Photo: Self Portrait
Cover Design: Elizabeth Maines McCleavy

Order online: www.finishinglinepress.com
also available on amazon.com

Author inquiries and mail orders:
Finishing Line Press
PO Box 1626
Georgetown, Kentucky 40324
USA

Table of Contents

EXTRANJERA

Crossings 1

ROOTS 2

La Posada del Sol 3

Escaping the Bonds 4

Fotografias 5

American Immigrant 6

Glass Doors 7

MUJER

Morena 11

Value 12

Courage 13

Gendered 14

Two Men Walking a Breast 15

Wide-Eyed 16

Delicate Fouls 17

ARTISTA

An Artist's Argument 21

the lazy 22

Songbird 23

Caged Serendipity 24

Expectations 25

Silver Linings 26

Mourning Doves 27

EXTRANJERA

Crossings

Intersections that are
forged in obstacles

Drawn to the fringes
of ambivalence

Compressed into
fragments

Underlying the
structures

That justified
communal suffering

Inherited pain with
brown eyes and skin.

ROOTS

I come from black volcanic ash
Barren of trees, lacking vegetation and civilization
(desolate and unproductive like society during the pandemic)

I come from hardworking
Tough-loving, tenderhearted dark women
and short, guttered reckless men,
carpenters, welders, handymans, men of all work
With skin shades ranging from
Common mango yellow to
Cold-pressed dark cacao.

I am barren of patience,
quietly waiting for an impending rupture,
Like the Cerro Negro that raised me.

Italicized portion is from Donna Weir-Soley's *First Rain*, poem of the same title.

La Posada del Sol

The cement bricks were chiseled gray and stained, with life crashing over it. Every year,
summer came and everything was exactly as I left it when I returned. I grinned so hard the sweat
rolled right into my little lips. We played smack in the middle of the road. This was my
street, *mi callejon*. *La Posada del Sol* whispered stories, from that one time the neighborhood
loco fell and cracked his skull to the hundred times I skinned an elbow. The brightness drained
me each day until I turned full raisin. Yet, my sweaty palms never gave up playing and my knees
bled on those dirty bricks. More than once. But I was too cool, *no es nada,* I would swear and
wipe the dirt off my wounds. At night we would sit, *piernas cruzadas* on the blocks listening to
my Abuela tell stories of boys and girls taken away by *la Llorona,* if they stayed out past curfew.
When August came, I knew it was over. The ceremonial tears fell on the *la Posada del Sol*, not
knowing that I would never return after my *quinces*. A mirage of memories left on that road.

Escaping the Bonds

a collection of stories that encompass the elusive fragmented identity
diving into tradition and challenges of preconceived notions about
exile
woven in carefully, defined through experience of being
composed of its own accord, through the loss of home
wandering in life and startling themselves when faced with how it all
began
and yet provide a glimpse of the labyrinths of recognition
continuously attempting to liberate itself
from the contrasting ideals of moderation and success
decimating the labels of the other
bonded by experience alone

Fotografias

Worn-down artifacts, collected candid snippets,
her experience as a mother, daughter and wife,
a reminder of simpler times, source of comfort,
igniting joy in her soul, simply by turning a page.

Dusted dirt floors surrounded by tin walls,
bright striped Guess shirts and denim,
wide jeans and even brighter smiles,
siblings through it all, *ternura profunda.*

The lens used to capture a culture and journey,
life bound together by a thin slither of plastic.
Memories that do not illustrate the struggles,
but rather encapsulate the joy.

American Immigrant

I pledge allegiance to this nation, that never thought I belonged here. As a citizen I accept my path into assimilation, learning the history and bloodshed. My truth cannot be tarnished. My culture will never be erased. I, too am American by default. That answer never suffices. I pledge allegiance to my people, those silenced and oppressed fighting for another chance. My voice demands attention, the rights I have been given but do not belong to my parents. Under God, I vow to seek my own equity, so that my liberty could bring justice to them all. One nation, torn by the Americans who refuse to share their independence with those in need of refuge. Invisible and irrelevant to their changing policies because I was merely born here. Neither immigrant nor American. Liberty and justice for all, except we exclude the immigrants seeking refuge and peace. Responsible for the laws I do not comprehend but do not apply to me. A prisoner of freedom burdened to ask for changes to be made.

Glass Doors

Walking through doors my mother worked so hard to hold open
Her knuckles bare from the pressure, fingertips pulsating
Shoulders hunched and exhausted
"Pasa mi Nena" she whispers

Mujer

Morena

Past the dominos aged men,
making ends meet by scrubbing the floors
of others, breathing in the spices and curry.
Relative but scarce like temperature under 80.

Accelerating at body language & philanthropy,
without learning boundaries.
Learning that sensuality is a prowess.
Never taking for granted running water and lighting.

Cluttered heritage hidden behind pride.
Governed by assimilation instead of mindfulness,
lucky to simply be accepted in society.
Life as a Latina firstborn into a new civilization.

Adapting into the wreckage of a country born of disparities.
A diaspora enabled by righteousness,
samples of selflessness dipped into desperation,
recreating the meaning of sacrifice.

Defining the term as selfish idealism,
unable to express the depression of consumption.
Purposefully hiding feelings of anxiety to avoid tension,
La vida es una bendición says Abuela.

Value

If there is one thing in my city that is powerful,
it is the ability to sit and smile when told.

Courage

Pleasure is this palpable sin
consuming the flesh

Devouring purity and diminishing value
perplexing the mind

Condemning the sensations
and nurture of sex

Gendered

From conception we
are inevitably
gendered

Showered in gifts
representing male or
female

Given toys that
encapsulate
consumerist retail

Baby blue ball caps
and pretty pink
princesses

Every aspect of
identity tailored to a
gender

Two Men Walking a Breast
Or Things that might get you sexually harassed

Walking down the street.
Walking down the street in a dress.
Walking down a crowded street.

Being Latina, White,
Asian, African.
Having blue eyes,
having brown eyes.

Going to a bar and buying a drink,
with your friends,
with your boyfriend.

Trying to help someone out at work.
Working out or standing alone,
anywhere.

Riding a bike in broad daylight.
Having long hair or short hair.
Being young, being old.

Having breasts.
Having large breasts.
Not having breasts at all.

Ask yourself:
How long do I want to live?
How can I do things differently?
What am I doing wrong?

Italicized portion is from Maureen Seaton's *Sweet World*, poem of the same title.

Wide-Eyed

And how long does a woman spend dying?
Perhaps from the womb, she came despaired?
Will she carry the equity of her gender?
Does that weight die with time?
Do her gentle eyes shy away from the center?
Does she stay still, just seconds or for millions of years, wide-eyed?
How does she retain her breathe in that instant?
Is she breathing at all?
Will she feel her bosom collapse into her chest?
Or does it sit, like the pressure and burden of existence?
Do her ambitions still cause her voice to tremble?
And do they still shout the revenge she never kept?
Will she scream in silence or echo?
Can anyone hear her at all?
Will she finally release her grief, lay it open and bare?
Do her words escape into the universe?
How long does she withstand the brutality?
Was it painful?
Does she feel the tenderness behind memories? It is sweet?
Can she still determine her fate, in those spare moments?
Will she stay etched, like a taint of color in a painting?
Stitched in a stranger's mind?
Does it last for eternity?
What does it mean to say "for ever"?

Inspired by Pablo Neruda

Delicate Fouls

Devoid stares
Oils of tension
Pull of apprehension
Defined by desires
Delicate fouls of attraction
Pretentious rules of seduction

Artista

An Artist's Argument

but what defines an art form?
A painting, lyrical notes, the emotion behind a concept?

Writing itself serves
as a supplement to speech but it is taken as an elementary skill.

Described as singular work,
lonely and fulfilled immediately. Writing is itself complex,

it is a mode of expression.
A form of thinking rhetorically and allowing the mind to wander

in physical text.
To write is to think. Think about the audience,

context, shifting ideas and concepts.
Experience and patience are required of a writer. Everyone can write

but not everyone can write well.
The rhetorical situation dictates everything, and experience is what allows

the writer to sit and revise.
It is an art form to sit and produce a novella or script,

it is storytelling
at its finest and it is most certainly never lonely.

the lazy

The amateur sits grazing his chin,
stuck to the stained faux leather chair,
obese with blank pages.

Weighing in on conversations,
Stealing plot lines and clever character flaws.
Waiting and indulging this idea of inspirations.

Disguising his inability to produce,
a self-taught procrastinator.

Songbird

I waited everyday
in the pale blue hues

Each night passed
I never waned

It would come to me
my little songbird

To whisper the bliss
of inspiration

Pure light direct
from heaven above

I became tall and static
hesitating in the silence

Open mouthed and still
until it came

The realization
it started in my temples

It crept into my walls
waivered my spirit

Until my core was
the only thing left

Inspiration was a myth
it did not exist

With the dirt under my nails
I had to revise

Caged Serendipity

          fortune
              told
                    fragile
              bird
         fenced
inward

Expectations

                          Sweetness is the bitter part of the memory
                    A tainted kiss that left my mouth bare
           Reckless to believe in the signs I created
      Dumbfounded at the result
Reality is never expected

Silver Linings

Fixated on designs clouded in pure intentions
forecasting life through an aged circumstance
hiding the embers of past aggressions

Mourning Doves

"What are those?" she asked delicately, each word elongated.
"Those are mourning doves" she replied, clinging to each word.
"Do you only see them during the day?" she pondered; the pensive creature waited for a reply. She shook her head and whisked her child out of the park. She walked away in a brisk manner and with each step she felt that ache, trembling. Breathing hesitantly, she kept thinking of her fowls, questioning why she shouldn't teach her daughter of these agents of memory. That evening when she tucked her birdie into bed, she caressed her forehead and whispered…
"No, quite frankly I see them all the time… you will too…"

Jennifer Mariela Rivera is a graduate from Florida International University, where she studied English Education. As a student, she developed a passion for writing and penned her first published chapbook, *La Interseccion*. She was born and raised in the diverse Miami, Florida but her parents came to the United States from Puerto Rico and Nicaragua. It became second nature to write poetry in English and Spanish due to her environment. Her poems are divided by different perspectives and emphasize the intersections of identity caused by her surroundings. Her poetry is stemmed from personal experiences and inspired by poets like Donna Weir-Soley, Maureen Seaton, and John Murillo. She is an educator and a poet. As she teaches at a non-profit private school in Homestead, FL, she is simultaneously working on her second chapbook. She lives in Miami, FL, with her husband and two dogs Zeus and Luna.

www.ingramcontent.com/pod-product-compliance
Lightning Source LLC
LaVergne TN
LVHW041512070426
835507LV00012B/1515